MW01714354

THE WAY OUT

The Story of NONIA

1920 - 1990

THE WAY OUT

The Story of NONIA

1920 - 1990

Edgar House

Creative Publishers
St. John's, Newfoundland
1990

The publisher acknowledges the financial contribution of the *Cultural Affairs Division of the Department of Municipal and Provincial Affairs, Government of Newfoundland and Labrador*, which has helped make this publication possible.

Cover design and illustration by Sphinx Rising

∝ Printed on acid-free "Sno Glo" Offset paper

Printed in Canada by:
ROBINSON-BLACKMORE PRINTING & PUBLISHING LTD.
P.O. Box 8660, St. John's, Newfoundland A1B 3T7

Published by
CREATIVE PUBLISHERS
A Division of Robinson-Blackmore Printing & Publishing Ltd.
P.O. Box 8660, St. John's, Newfoundland A1B 3T7

Canadian Cataloguing in Publication Data

House, Edgar, 1911–

The way out

ISBN 0-920021-90-5

1. Newfoundland Outport Nursing and Industrial Association — History. 2. Handicraft industries — Newfoundland — History. I. Title.

HD2346.C32N54 1990 338.7'68'09718 C91-097508-6

DEDICATION

TO THE
MANY DEDICATED NURSES
OF
O.N.C. and NONIA

WHO EXCHANGED
THE
COMPARATIVE COMFORTS
OF
GREAT BRITAIN

FOR
THE RUGGED CONDITIONS
OF THE
NEWFOUNDLAND OUTPORTS
OF THE
TWENTIES AND THIRTIES

AND
THERE ESTABLISHED A STANDARD
OF
RURAL NURSING SERVICES
WHICH
HAS NOWHERE BEEN SURPASSED

ALSO
TO THE FARSIGHTED FOUNDERS OF NONIA

AND
TO THE MANY DEVOTED
STAFF MEMBERS
AND VOLUNTEERS

WHOSE DONATIONS OF
TIME, TALENTS, AND DOLLARS
INITIALLY HELPED TO SUPPORT THE NURSES
AND SUBSEQUENTLY ENABLED
MANY HUNDREDS OF KNITTERS AND WEAVERS
TO SUSTAIN A BETTER STANDARD OF LIVING
IN THEIR HOMES.

Contents

Foreword

by

Mrs. Phyllis Winter

(President of Nonia 1966-1980)

With mixed feelings, I accept this opportunity to introduce to you this very complete history of Nonia only because I'm the one who has been associated with Nonia for almost all of its seventy years, through my mother and then because of my own deep interest.

I mind having to accept the fact that I have become almost a relic but my great satisfaction has come from the group of young women whom I feel I was able to attract to the Nonia Committee; now its success is entirely because of their up-to-date approach to business as it is done nowadays.

I sincerely hope that they will derive the same satisfaction from their association as I have. Without the involvement and dedication over the years of the staff, the knitters and the weavers, who have always known that Nonia standards are our most important asset, we could never have survived. For seventy years, Nonia has been fortunate in its many wonderful friends and its great success is, in part, due to their support. We have always had a feeling of being a contributor to the women of Newfoundland in opening up an area for them to be able to help towards the family income, while, at the same time, being at home with their families.

I think the research Mr. House has put into this history is an edification for those unfamiliar with Nonia's background and I thank him most sincerely for perpetuating our interesting story.

Preface

Several months ago I was asked (by a member of the Board of Nonia) whether I would consider compiling a history of the seventy year old Association.

At that time, I was busily trying to complete another project but, when told that "there was no great hurry," I readily volunteered to help.

I have always had great admiration for what Nonia has done and is doing and, since I started researching the records, this has deepened.

The dedication at the front (of this volume) adequately expresses my feeling towards Nonia. It is an honour to have been asked to record one of the finest chapters in our island story.

On the Fiftieth Anniversary of Nonia in 1970, a writer in "Trade Talk" magazine referred to Nonia as "one of the most durable organizations in Newfoundland." Now, twenty years later at age seventy, Nonia is still hale and hearty; may it continue to be "durable" in the Nineties and into the fast approaching Twenty First Century.

Edgar House

Acknowledgements

The author is greatly indebted to so many individuals that to try to name all of them is to risk omitting some. All have been individually thanked and, if a name or two is omitted below, I hope it will be regarded as faulty memory and not ingratitude.

My thanks, then, are extended to:
Lucy Burrage
Florence Chafe
Frances Clarke
Pamela Dawe
Bill Guihan
Cecil Hookey
Jeannie House
Everett Hudson
David Leaman (A.C. Hunter Library)
Loretta Martin
Joyce Nevitt
Evelyn Power *(Evening Telegram)*
Ian Reid
Valda Tiller
Janice Udell (Cover)
Phyllis Winter
Marilyn Woolridge

My special thanks go to Sydney Anne Ryan who bravely volunteered to decipher the products of my shaky hand and transform them into error-free type.

E.G.H.

The Title

From the beginning of his long service as a medical missionary in Fortune Bay, Rev. H.J.A. MacDermott was deeply concerned about the appalling living conditions of the people in the various settlements which he visited. In his biography he records the advice of a well-known preacher, who once said, "Don't ever try to preach to people whose feet are cold and whose stomachs are empty." Throughout his long ministry in Fortune Bay, this remarkable man and his wife worked tirelessly for the physical and spiritual well being of the people.

When, in 1924, Lady Allardyce, convinced that Nonia could become self-supporting, received the first supplies of wool and patterns it was natural for her to turn to a very depressed area such as Fortune Bay in which to try them; it was also natural for her to seek the help of Rev. MacDermott in organizing a meeting of the men and women of the area.

So, in late June, Rev. MacDermott was delighted to receive a telegram from Sir William Allardyce requesting him to do this. Much later, in his memoirs, Rev. MacDermott recorded "I did not see for some time that this was "The Way Out," through an opening door of which that telegram was the first sound of the lifting latch."

Nonia indeed became "The Way Out" not only for scores of families in Fortune Bay but also for hundreds in outports on all our coasts.

It is, therefore, most fitting that the words of Rev. MacDermott, the most outstanding of all Nonia supporters, should be the title for the story of Nonia.

Greetings from

Honourable
Margaret McGrath

Honourary Patroness of Nonia

I am delighted to respond to the invitation of Mr. Edgar House to be part of this commemorative book. Mr. House provides us with a dedicated work, a delightful and memorable journey of one of Newfoundland's pioneer adventures in entrepreneurship.

NONIA, initially a dream of one of my predecessors in this office, directly and concretely addressed a suffering people in the outports of our province. These great women who formed this association risked "for a dream". With the spirit of cooperation amongst our outport people, the dream became a reality in Government House in 1925 when the constitution of NONIA was drawn up. Twelve years later Her Majesty the Queen granted permission for NONIA to use the words "as supplied to Her Majesty the Queen".

Our challenge today is to respond to Mr. Edgar House's book to help keep this dream alive by retelling the story. This is a marvellous and unique contribution to our pioneer history. I am grateful to be part of the dream come true—to be a part of the great tapestry of Newfoundland history.

Margaret McGrath, O.St.J., BSc. (Hons.)

Lady Elsie Allardyce
1924–1929

Lady Mabel Middleton
1929–1932

Lady Anderson
1932–1936

Lady Eileen Walwyn
1936–1944

Mrs. C.E.A. Jeffery
1945–1946

Mrs. Harold Mitchell
Vice-President 1945-1946
President 1946–1958

The Presidents

of NONIA

(1924 – 1990)

Mrs. Annabella Baird
1958–1960

Lady Outerbridge
1960–1966

Mrs. Phyllis Winter
1966–1981

Mrs. Karen Hickman
1981–1985

Mrs. Valda Tiller
1985–

Chapter One

(1920-24)

Introduction

IN ORDER to place in true perspective the great contribution made by the Newfoundland Outport Nursing and Industrial Association, it is necessary to picture the conditions in Newfoundland as they were shortly after World War I, 1914-18.

In his history of Newfoundland (1958), Mr. A. B. Perlin recorded that "the worst depression in Newfoundland's history up to that time fell on the country with devastating force."

It was also a period of great political instability.

Picture then the government of a small impoverished island of 42,700 square miles trying to serve the needs of a population of 263,000 living in approximately 1,300 settlements scattered along a coastline of more than 6000 miles; there were few roads and none were paved. The sea was the highway.

In all, there were only 45 doctors, mostly in St. John's and the larger towns; from Hermitage to Port aux Basques, a distance of 150 miles, there were 6,500 residents but not one doctor or nurse!

Public hospitals were non-existent apart from the General Hospital, the Lunatic Asylum (now the Water-ford) and the Tuberculosis Sanatorium—all located in St. John's—and those operated in the North by the International Grenfell Association.

Even in the Capital, conditions were so deplorable that, thanks largely to the 1916 report of Dr. R. A. Brehm, Medical Officer of Health, and the concern and generosity of Mayor W. G. Gosling and Lady Davidson, wife of the Governor, the Child Welfare Association was born in 1917.

The urgency of the situation was obvious from the fact that, in St. John's in 1920, the infant mortality rate per 1000 live births was 146.34.

The aim of the Child Welfare Association was well expressed in its motto "To Keep Well Babies Well."

The Work of Lady Harris

In 1917, Lady Harris replaced Lady Davidson as chatelaine at Government House. On June 20, 1920, she formally opened the Child Welfare Centre in the Public

Courtesy of Garland Studio

Shocking conditions of ignorance and poverty in St. John's, 1920

Health Building and soon came to have a good realization of the shocking conditions of ignorance and poverty as they pertained to public health in the capital city.

Outport Conditions Even More Appalling

However, it was not till Lady Harris made several trips around the island with her husband that she realized the even greater need that there was for medical

Lady Harris

Mrs. Evelyn Cave Hiscock, R.N.

and nursing services in all outports; the infant mortality rate was shocking.

Nurse Evelyn Hiscock of the staff of the General Hospital, through several visits to different outports, was also deeply concerned about what she had observed.

The Outport Nursing Committee of 1920

Both ladies met on several occasions and, as a result of their planning, the Outport Nursing Committee was formed on May 27, 1920.

There were five members on the original committee as follows:

Chairman: Hon. Dr. Alex Campbell
Secretary and Treasurer: Lady Harris
Mr. R. A. Squires
Hon. W. W. Halfyard
Rev. Edgar Jones

Hon. A Campbell, M.D., Chairman

The Committee was approved by Minute of Council and the Government agreed to provide a grant to assist in paying the salary of specially trained nurses.

Very shortly afterwards, Lady Harris visited England and sought the help of the Overseas Nursing Association in finding well-qualified nurses, preferably those with experience in midwifery. Six were engaged almost immediately and, within a few months, they had opened nursing centres at Rose Blanche, Hodge's Cove, Daniel's Harbour, Joe Batt's Arm, Lower Island Cove and Hant's Harbour.

The salaries of these six nurses, all of whom had signed two-year contracts, were made up chiefly of Government grants. It was intended and hoped that patients would contribute towards services received

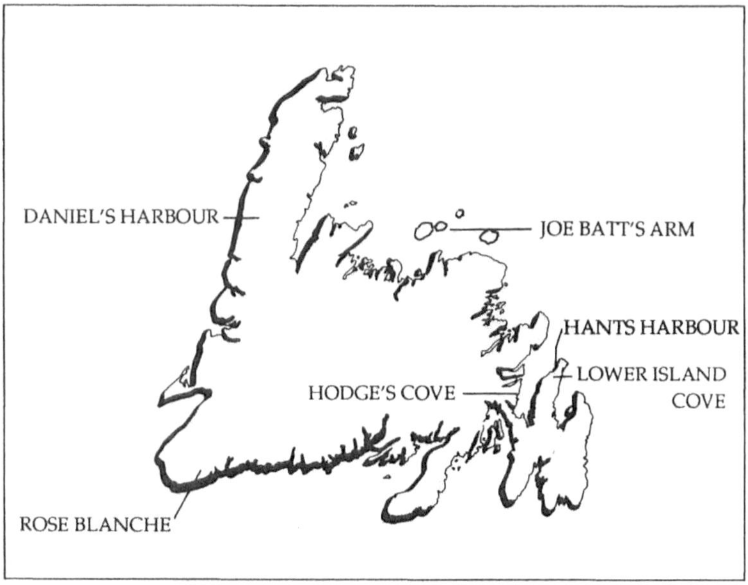

The first six Outport Nursing Committee centres

and that the scheme would soon prove to be self-supporting.

Unfortunately, by 1922, two of the O.N.C. members had left Newfoundland. Lady Harris, whose husband's term as Governor had expired, returned to England and Rev. Edgar Jones of St. Thomas' Church, moved to the United States.

Three of the six nurses had married and another suffered a physical breakdown after her first year of work. Apparently no steps were taken to replace either the Committee members or the nurses whose contract had expired.

It must also be remembered that the post-war conditions referred to earlier made the financial positions of the outport people so bad that money for food, clothing and shelter had to take precedence over fees to support a nurse.

The "barter system" was also prevalent in most outports. The merchant outfitted the fishermen in the spring and received fish as payment in the fall; if, after the "squaring up" was completed, there was anything left it was used to lay in provisions for the winter; if extremely lucky, the men received some cash as final payment. Generally speaking, however, little money was in circulation and donations to charity were scarce.

The Impact of Lady Elsie Allardyce

The whole Outport Nursing Committee movement was "in the doldrums" and it took several months for the new Governor's wife, Lady Elsie Allardyce, to realize the great importance of the work which had been initiated by her predecessor. However, when she

Honourary President and Founder,
Lady Elsie E. Allardyce
(April 3, 1924)

did, her enthusiasm was so unlimited and infectious that the outport nursing movement benefitted for years from the impetus that she gave it. Jim Thoms, in his excellent brief history of Nonia, in 1970, wrote that "Lady Allardyce dived into the work."

From the beginning, Lady Allardyce was convinced that the outport nursing movement could become self-supporting. Fortunately, she had some knowledge of the way by which the women of the Shetland and Fayre Islands of Scotland had been able to organize their labour during World War I in knitting garments for the men of the armed forces. Following the Armistice, they continued their knitting as a cottage industry and, with diversified patterns, found a ready market for their products.

Lady Allardyce, through her many contacts, was able to obtain samples of the Scottish garments as well as many patterns. A supply of wool was purchased and this, with the patterns and sample garments, was brought to Fortune Bay by Lady Allardyce when she accompanied Sir William on a visit to the South Coast. At that time, Fortune Bay was one of the most distressed areas in Newfoundland. The women of Pool's Cove and other nearby settlements showed a keen interest and were soon producing marketable garments of excellent quality. It became apparent that the women of Fortune Bay would be able to earn enough to help their families and also to contribute towards the salary of a nurse.

It was at this point that Lady Allardyce and her Committee decided to call a public meeting in St. John's and invite all interested persons to attend and, hopefully, form an association.

Chapter Two

(1924-1934)

NONIA is Born

ON JANUARY 24, 1924, in Canon Wood Hall, the Outport Nursing Committee convened a public meeting which was well attended by representatives of Church and State as well as the general citizenry.

The Chairmen was Prime Minister W. R. Warren and, such was the enthusiasm that a large number of volunteers and members, both male and female, was enrolled.

A few months later, on April 3rd, after careful planning, a meeting was held at Government House and the Newfoundland Outport Nursing and Industrial Association was officially founded. The Executive Committee was as follows:

Hon. President (and Founder):	Lady Elsie Allardyce
Hon. Vice Presidents:	The wife of the Prime Minister (ex-officio) The wife of the Mayor (ex-officio) Mrs. Wm. White (Bishop's Court) Mrs. Cluny Macpherson

Hon. Association Secretary:	Mrs. W. R. Warren
Hon. Nursing Secretary:	Miss Loder
Hon. Industrial Secretary:	Mrs. H. B. Mitchell
Hon. Treasurer:	Mr. Geo. R. Cake
Acting Hon. Treasurer:	Mr. T. V. Harnett

Committee Members: Rev. Canon Bolt, Miss Myra Taylor, Dr. T. M. Mitchell, Mr. W. W. Halfyard, Hon. S. Milley, Lady Squires, Miss May Furlong

The O.N.C. and NONIA Nurses (1920-1934)

The contribution to the health and welfare of thousands of outport people by the forty-five Nonia nurses from 1920 to 1934 must never be forgotten.

The first of six nurses, Casement and Smith, were engaged by Lady Harris while on a visit to England; she was greatly assisted in their selection by the Overseas Nursing Association in London. These nurses arrived in St. John's with Lady Harris in October, 1920.

Shortly before their arrival, Nurse Button, a Newfoundlander, was sent to Lead Cove, Trinity Bay, where she served for a short period.

By the spring of 1921, several other nurses began to arrive including Myra Grimsley who went to Daniel's Harbour where she soon married. As Mrs. Angus Bennett, she continued to work for many years and her outstanding career merits a separate volume.

Each nurse signed a two-year contract in which she agreed that, in addition to the ordinary nursing duties, she would undertake to serve as a midwife without the assistance of a doctor. Most of the nurses chosen by the Overseas Nursing Association already had training in midwifery; if not, they were advised to take special courses before leaving for Newfoundland.

Detailed monthly reports were to be submitted and a one month annual holiday was granted. The salary

Nurse Casement, Rose Blanche, 1920

Nurse Smith, Hodge's Cove, 1920

Nurse Harvey, Joe Batt's Arm, 1921

Newfoundland Nurse Rose

SOME OF THE FIRST NURSES

Pictures of nurses Courtesy of *The Newfoundland Quarterly*

Nurse Myra (Grimsley) Bennett M.B.E., O.C., D.Sc.(Hon) M.U.N., O.N.C. Nurse 1921-1923, voluntary nurse 1923-1934, Dept. of Health nurse 1934-53 and retirement nurse for many years at Daniel's Harbour where she died in April, 1990 at age 100 years.

was $900, $75 per month, a fairly attractive figure at that time.

Many nurses renewed their contract after two years and their impact on the areas in which they served was remarkable. Several, for health reasons, were forced to discontinue. One of these was found to have contracted tuberculosis in the line of duty and died within a few years after her return to England.

It is fitting that the names of these forty-five nurses should be recorded.

*Battock	Dempster	Lloyd-Acton	Ryan
Beeston	Dougall	Martin	Seaman
Budsby	Edwards	Mayer	Smith
*Button	Grimsley	Meikle	*Spracklin
Campbell	(Bennett)	McKeague	Waller
Casement	Grimshaw	McMahon	Weeks
Cherry	Hainsworth	MacDonald	Weir
Cleghorn	Hore	Noble	Welch
*Costello	Hughes	Phillips	Wheaton
Crabb	Johnson	Robinson	Wild
Currant	King	*Rose	Winnal
Davies	Layton	Ruffle	

*from Newfoundland, serving mostly as relief nurses for short periods.

Nursing Centres
(1924 – 1934)

In 1925, it was decided that any community, large or small, that wished to become a part of Nonia must form a local committee of at least five members.

From these should be elected a President, Vice-President, and Secretary or Secretary-Treasurer. It was the responsibility of the Committee, usually through the Secretary, to:

a. receive the wool and instructions
b. distribute these to knitters
c. return finished goods to the Depot
d. distribute the payment cheques to the workers

It was hoped that each Committee would be able to raise seventy-five per cent of the nurse's salary; the other twenty-five per cent would be paid by the Government. Each Committee signed a contract with Nonia before a nurse was assigned to the area.

The following twenty-eight centres were served for varying periods from 1921 to 1934:

Bay L'Argent, 1930
Burgeo, 1929
Coachman's Cove, 1925
Daniel's Harbour, 1921
Eastport, 1930
Flat Island, B.B., 1930
Fleur-de-Lys, 1925
Garnish, 1924
Grand Bank, 1931
Green's Harbour, 1927
Hant's Harbour, 1921
Hodge's Cove, 1921
Jackson's Arm, 1925
Joe Batt's Arm
Lamaline, 1929
La Scie, 1925
Long Island, 1929
Lower Island Cove, 1921
Port Saunders, 1921
Port Union & Catalina
Pouch Cove, 1924
Ramea, 1928
Rencontre West, 1929
Rose Blanche, 1921
Salvage, 1930
Sop's Arm, 1925
St. Joseph's, 1926
White Bay South
(Seal Cove, Western Arm, Westport, 1927)

Even after the Nursing side of Nonia was terminated in 1934, a number of new centres were formed; a few, for various reasons including the resettlement program, dropped out.

The Work of the *Overseas Nursing Association,* London

It is doubtful whether, without the invaluable services of the Overseas Nursing Association of London, England, NONIA of Newfoundland could have survived.

Lady Owen, an executive member of O.N.A., showed a great personal interest in the selection of the nurses who were to serve in Newfoundland. The selection committee took great pains to choose nurses who were not only *physically fit* to cope with the tough climatic conditions of Newfoundland, but who also showed, in their interviews, that they were *"missionary" minded.*

The fantastic record of the NONIA nurses is positive proof that the O.N.A. selection committee did an outstanding job in choosing the nurses who signed contracts to serve, for varying periods, from 1920 to 1934.

The London Committee of Nonia

In the first Nonia Annual Report, July 27, 1925, Lady Allardyce reported that "a London committee of Newfoundlanders had recently been formed with Mrs. Amery, the wife of the Secretary of State for Dominion Affairs, as the first member."

The officers were:

Hon. President:	The High Commissioner of Newfoundland, Captain Victor Gordon

President: Mrs. George Emerson
Hon. Treasurer: Mrs. F. Kennedy
Hon. Secretary: Mrs. M. K. Baird

This group carried on till June, 1927, when a completely new slate of officers was elected, as follows:

President: Mrs. W. C. Job
Hon. Secretary: Mrs. Ramsay Green
Hon. Asst. Secretary: Mrs. G. Hawes
Hon. Treasurer: Miss Florence Nightingale

Miss Nightingale continued in office and sent annual financial reports to Nonia headquarters in St. John's until 1949; Mrs. Job also carried on as President.

Within a couple of years, the membership of the London branch reached nearly 80 and Captain Gordon and his staff were untiring in their efforts to advance the work of Nonia. The membership peaked to 122 in 1930 and then gradually dropped to about half that number at the time when the Commission of Government assumed responsibility for the nursing side of Nonia.

The 1926 Annual report records that the London Branch had sent the generous sum of £300 (£10 of which had been received from Her Majesty, the Queen.) This was the result of an appeal by Lady Allardyce who was convinced of the need of a trained Depot worker.

In late 1926, the London Committee decided to meet weekly to make all manner of useful articles, so that the Nonia nurses could be supplied with bags of clothing—a need which the committee in St. John's had been unable to meet.

After the nursing side of Nonia was discontinued in 1934, the London Committee found it difficult to maintain interest. Nevertheless, the faithful few, under the perennial president, Mrs. Edith Job, carried on; fortnightly sewing meetings were held and useful

Courtesy of Mr. Ian Reid

LONDON FRIENDS OF NONIA
(circa 1935)
l-r: Mr. W.C. Job, Mrs. G. Hawes, Mr. George Hawes, Mrs. W. C. Job, Miss Louise Reid.

second-hand clothing was collected for the needy centres.

All the London Committee's activities were in abeyance from 1939-1945 because of Britain's all-out efforts during World War II.

For some time, following the Armistice, it was very difficult to send money out of England and no annual reports from the London Committee were received after 1949.

Nonia's Corner Brook Branch

Quite early in Nonia's history, November, 1926, Corner Brook formed a branch which, for more than forty years, became a tower of strength to the St. John's Board of Directors.

Since the Corner Brook area was well served by resident doctors and nurses, a Nonia nurse was not needed there. The branch therefore agreed to assist in financing the Nonia nurse at Port Saunders, a large centre on the north west coast.

Through the generosity of Mr H.M.S. Lewin, Manager of the International Pulp and Paper Company, a large showcase was donated and set up for both display and sales purpose in the Company's Glynmill Inn; this very popular Inn became Nonia's headquarters in Corner Brook.

In 1926, the membership of this branch was 120; many of those who paid their membership fees were males.

The first annual report, submitted on September 14, 1927 showed a very satisfactory revenue, from sales and membership, of $2,800.

Apart from the sales of goods at the Inn to local customers, the Corner Brook members found an excellent outlet every summer when cruise ships visited. Sometimes booths were set up at the pier; on other occasions, as in 1939, "two members of the committee were on the wharf for the arrival of every ship and distributed advertising material to the passengers and directed them to the Glynmill Inn where the rest of the Committee was waiting to sell them goods."

The members of the Corner Brook Branch did far more than raise funds through dances, movies, and sell Nonia goods. They also sent, every Christmas, a hamper to the nurse at Port Saunders; with this there often went packing cases of clothing, books, magazines, fruit and cakes for distribution to the needy. In fact, the Port Saunders Centre was, to a large extent, supported by the Corner Brook Branch; the Port Saunders nurses felt that they had a home in Corner Brook where a warm welcome always awaited them when they visited.

Following the closing of all Nonia Nursing Centres in 1934, including Port Saunders, the Corner Brook

Branch continued to support the industrial work of the Association by serving as a sales outlet for the West Coast.

Each year for the next three decades the annual reports showed sales of several thousand dollars under the supervision of such dedicated workers as Mrs. Cliff Hierlihy and Mrs. Norman Hood.

For several years before the closing of the Glynmill Inn outlet, a sales manager, Mrs. Stuart Osmond, was employed by Nonia and worthwhile sales were made: in 1965, for instance, these totalled $4,625.00.

The *Inn* then underwent extensive refurbishing and changes. In the process Nonia lost the space for its display case and the forty-year-old sales outlet had to be discontinued.

So, at the 41st Annual Meeting of Nonia in St. John's it was recorded that "the Corner Brook Committee voted to disband and the possibilities for selling Nonia goods through an established retail outlet will be investigated."

This was done and, for a few months, the Royal Stores became the outlet for Nonia knitted and woven goods.

Among those who served as President of the Corner Brook Branch for varying periods from 1926 to 1965 were the following:

Mrs. J. P. McLaurin (9 years)
Mrs. E. Bernard Smith
Mrs. A. P. Ledingham
Mrs. F. P. Silver
Mrs. J. A. House (10 years)
Mrs. A. L. Ballock and
Mrs. Loretta Martin.

Chapter Three

The End of the Nursing Side of Nonia

IN THE FOURTEEN YEARS between the arrival of the first two Outport Committee Nurses in the Fall of 1920, until the Department of Health and Welfare assumed control of all the Colony's Nursing Services on September 30, 1934, an unforgettable chapter of bravery and devotion to duty was indelibly written in the history of nursing in Newfoundland.

For ten years after its foundation on April 10, 1924, Nonia continued to expand its good works and, by 1934, there were eight active centres—Argentia, Hant's Harbour, Garnish, Lamaline, Port Saunders, Rencontre West, Salvage, and White Bay.

In that year, 3,974 patients received treatment and 16,971 home visits were made by the dedicated nurses.

Commission of Government assumes control

In 1934 after less than two years of stewardship, the Commission of Government decided to assume control of *all* nursing services in Newfoundland.

On May 15 notification came to the Nonia Executive Committee from the Department of Health and Welfare that all records, books, nurses' contracts, drugs, and office equipment should be turned over to the Department.

The actual wording of the Resolution was as follows:

> Whereas the Newfoundland Government have notified the Association that all Nursing Services shall be administered by the Government and the grant of this Association shall cease:
>
> IT IS RESOLVED that such steps as may be necessary to transfer to the Government the administration of the Nursing Services at present carried out by this Association and that the __________________ are hereby authorized to effect such transfer accordingly.

By June 1, the eight nurses, record books, drugs etcetera, were all transferred to the Department of Health and Welfare, thus ending the primary purpose of Nonia; nevertheless, the Association continued to administer the Nursing Services, on behalf of the Government, until September 30 of that year.

27 outports had been served during Nonia's nursing years, during which 83,000 cases were treated and 232,000 home visits were made.

The Social, Cultural and Educational Benefits of the Nonia Nursing Centres

It is impossible to gauge the total impact of the many well-educated English Nonia nurses on the communities in which they worked.

In many happy "get togethers," while they chatted and knitted away at the garments required for the Depot, "much of the nurses' knowledge and culture must have rubbed off on those present."

Many of the nurses had newspapers, magazines and books sent to them from England, St. John's, and Corner Brook; these were eagerly looked at in the clinics or when circulated in the community. Those who were unable to read enjoyed the pictures from another world. Nurse Walker wrote from Port Saunders in 1928 to say "I have been able to start a little lending library with all the books and papers so kindly sent out by Mrs. Murray and Mrs. David Baird. One feels glad for anything that will break the monotony for the people in these isolated places."

Several of the nurses had some musical training and initiated, or participated in, concerts and "times" in school rooms, church halls or lodges; a few had been Girl Guides in England and sponsored, or assisted in setting up, a company in their centre.

In 1927 Nurse MacDonald at White Bay South found time, in spite of making 5,553 home visits and seeing more than 800 patients in that year, to use her Magic Lantern in giving illustrated health talks and to show a popular set of slides, "Alice in Wonderland," to groups of children.

Tales of Adventure and Devotion (1920-1934)

Trained in a much kinder climate where travel was relatively easy, the Nonia nurses had to adapt themselves to commuting long distances by means of "shank's mare," snow-shoes, dog team, and open boats, often in rough and sub-zero weather.

That our rugged coast made a vivid impression can be seen from the following extract from an early letter received at H.Q. in St. John's from Nurse Johnston, stationed at Rencontre West. Describing a visit to Cul-de-Sac, she wrote that it was "not unlike a huge cave—only seventy yards across the harbour—so rocky that, if an inhabitant dies, the body has to be brought to New Harbour, several miles distant, for burial."

The following stories come from various sources, mostly Nonia annual reports.

In Open Boat

(i) "In 1931, Nurse McDonald of Westport, White Bay, endured twenty-four hours of exposure in an open motor boat while taking a critically ill patient to St. Anthony Hospital."

(ii) "One nurse was grounded in an open boat off Garnish for nearly two hours expecting, at any moment, to be swamped by heavy seas and high winds."

On "Shank's Mare"

Lady Middleton reported, in 1932, that "in one of our most difficult districts last February in zero weather our Nurse MacDonald, when it was impossible to get a dog team, went twice in one fortnight, on foot, from one end of her district to the other—a distance of about forty miles each way.

Another nurse was walking across a bay, when she fell through. Dragged out by her companions, she walked the remaining four miles in sub-zero weather in freezing, wet clothing.

On Snowshoes

(i) At Westport, W.B., Nurse Martin travelled about six miles over an unbroken trail the first time she put on snowshoes.

(ii) "One nurse tramped 14 miles through swirling snowdrifts the first time on snowshoes; three men beat the path for her and helped her to make it to the home of her patient."

Beyond the Call of Duty

"One of our nurses was in bed for five days with a badly scalded face and feared that her sight might be affected. An aluminum hot water bottle had burst in her face.

When called to attend to a sick woman and her child, the nurse wore a mask and was led to the house by the husband. She would not leave to be led home until she was assured of the safety of both her patients.

The Florence Nightingale of Lamaline

Following the Tidal Wave Disaster of November 29, 1929, Nurse Dorothy Cherry, stationed at Burin, did such remarkable work in her district that she was specially recognized by the Nonia directors. At a reception in Government House, she was presented with a beautiful silver clock. On that occasion, Dr. Mosdell, Minister of Health, referred to her as the "Florence Nightingale of the Tidal Wave Disaster." Later, when her story reached the New York papers, an admirer sent $350 to purchase a car. With this, in 1931, she was able to make 6,153 visits, a Nonia record.

Nurses, Pharmacists, Doctors or Dentists?

The Nonia nurses from Great Britain performed conscientiously all the duties that have come to be associated with nursing. Many of them kept "surgery" hours and spent the rest of the long working day making home visits.

Nurse Wild at Green's Harbour, reporting in 1928, wrote "I have surgery hours from 9 am to 11 am, when medicines are dispensed and all minor dressings, extractions, etc. are done. At 11 o'clock, I begin my rounds in the district—all midwifery and acute cases being attended to first. From 4 pm to 6 pm I am in the surgery again."

Their normal nursing care included attending to sprains, bruises and breaks, lancing boils, removing fish-hooks, stitching up wounds, and trying to control epidemics of flu or typhoid. In addition, they tried to teach the principles of hygiene and the rules of health, both formally and informally.

In her well-researched book, *White Caps and Black Bands,* author Joyce Nevitt records that "Nonia nurses were independent practitioners who performed many medical functions from sheer necessity and under very difficult conditions."

Midwifery

Because of her great interest and enthusiasm Lady Owen, President of the Overseas Nursing Association in London saw to it that, whenever possible, Nonia nurses had special training in midwifery before serving in Newfoundland. This extra training paid off and hundreds of babies were safely delivered in the twenty-seven Nonia Nursing Centres; scores of outport women were trained to assist.

While there were many difficult deliveries, one special one stands out very clearly. Nurse Cherry of Tidal Wave Disaster fame, realized on one occasion that only a Caesarean section could save the life of her patient. With the help of the local priest who acted as anaesthetist, Miss Cherry was able to perform the operation successfully.

Dentistry

Since there was only a handful of dentists in the Newfoundland of the twenties and thirties, many of the Nonia nurses became quite proficient in extracting teeth.

The 1932 Annual Report of Nonia records that, at Eastport, "Nurse Noble has extracted nearly 700 teeth since her arrival just a year ago."

In 1935, the year in which she received the King George V Medal for her good work at Daniel's Harbour, the late Myra (Grimsley) Bennett recorded that, up to that time, a period of thirteen years, she had extracted "around 3,000 teeth."

During her lifetime of service she is also credited with delivering more than 3,000 babies.

Chapter Four

The Industrial Side of Nonia

THE TWO-FOLD concept of Nonia as envisaged by Lady Allardyce, was formally stated as follows:

1. To provide employment in those outports where a Nonia nurse was stationed so that the women might help to pay a share of the nurse's salary.
2. To raise the standard of living by increasing the earning power of each of the Nonia communities.

The two branches, Nursing and Industrial, worked side by side until 1929 when it was decided to set up separate committees to operate them.

Mrs. Harold Mitchell headed up the Industrial side and Mrs. Eleanor Macpherson (wife of Dr. Cluny, also an ardent supporter of Nonia) the Nursing side. This arrangement continued for the next five years.

When the nursing side of Nonia was terminated in 1934, there were some misgivings and uncertainty about the future of the ten year old Association. The nursing aspect of eight active Centres had been closed; however, all but two of these had remained active as Industrial Centres. By September, 1935, the number of these Centres had increased to a surprising 33.

As with the original Centres, each new Industrial Centre had to be properly organized with elected officers including a Secretary or, usually, a Secretary-

Treasurer who would be responsible for ordering and receiving supplies, distributing them, sending the finished goods to Head Quarters and, later, making the payments to the knitters and weavers.

Lady Allardyce's dream of "raising the standard of living by increasing the earning power of each of the Nonia communities " was being fulfilled.

Registered Trade Mark and Cable Address

At one of the early executive meetings at Government House, it was agreed, at the suggestion of Lady Allardyce, that the word NONIA would be the cable address of the Association. Derived from the first letters of the official name, Newfoundland Outport Nursing and Industrial Association, "NONIA" also became the Registered Trade Mark for all articles sold.

Soon the name became known throughout Newfoundland as a symbol of quality and satisfaction. Lady Allardyce even had visions of a yacht to be named M.V. "NONIA" that would visit all the nursing and industrial centres bringing ample supplies of medicine and wool and returning to St. John's with the finished products of knitters and weavers.

New Letterhead
(circa 1961)

"From Pillar to Post" (the many Nonia headquarters)

The earliest knitted goods from Nonia centres were sent to Government House for sorting and sales but this ceased in 1924, when a generous friend offered temporary space.

#1 – The Reid-Newfoundland Building

Through the generosity of Mr. W. Angus Reid, Nonia's first depot, a temporary one, was located in the Reid-Newfoundland Building on Duckworth Street. Opened in the Spring of 1924, it was soon realized that there was insufficient space to display and store goods. It was also apparent that, even though there were many keen volunteers, a permanent secretary was essential.

#2 – The Exchange Building, Water Street

In 1925, rooms became available in the Exchange Building, on Water Street. Mr. W. I. Bishop of Montreal generously contributed $25 per month, for the first year, toward the rent. From this centre wool, patterns and

VISIT
THE "NONIA" SHOWROOM
WATER STREET, ST. JOHN'S
TWO DOORS WEST OF BANK MONTREAL

Here you will find a full assortment of hand knit SHETLAND WOOL Garments made by the Newfoundland fisherfolk.

CARDIGANS	SPORT DRESSES	GOLF STOCKINGS
JUMPERS	PULL OVERS	GLOVES
HOMESPUN TWEEDS		CHILDREN'S GARMENTS

— ORGANIZED BY —
THE NEWFOUNDLAND OUTPORT NURSING & INDUSTRIAL ASSOCIATION

To provide medical and nursing services for the Outports.

11 Nurses now serving under auspices of Association.

Take back a "NONIA" Nosegay with you!

weaving material were sent to 615 workers in 35 centres around the island.

#3 –The G.W.V.A. Building, Water Street

In early 1928, the Executive was successful in finding more spacious and suitable rooms in the Great War Veterans Association building, also on Water Street, and for five years, this depot served quite well.

#4 – The Newfoundland Hotel

In 1933, space became available at the popular Newfoundland Hotel where it was hoped that the patronage of tourists and travelling business people would lead to greater sales. The nerve centre of Nonia remained at this site for the next quarter century, when the old Newfoundland Hotel was torn down and replaced by the modern Hotel Newfoundland.

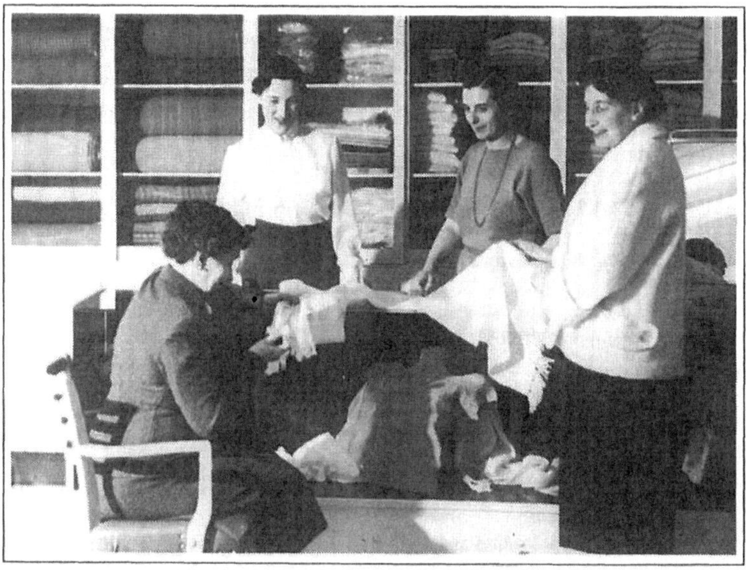

At NONIA H.Q. – NEWFOUNDLAND HOTEL (circa 1945)
Seated: Mrs. Boyd Baird
Standing: (l–r) Beatrice Hookey, Florence Chafe and Mrs. C.E.A. Jeffery.

#5 – The Sheffman Building, 286 Water Street

In January, 1958, after sound advice from an advisory committee consisting of Hon. Fabian O'Dea, Mr. Ian Reid and Hon. Treasurer Mr. E. Holmes, and after much renovation and alteration, #286 Water Street was leased. Fifteen years later, in 1973, the Association, again with expert advice, purchased the Sheffman building at 286 Water Street. Unfortunately, shortly after, an extensive fire occurred on St. Patrick's Day and considerable damage was done to both building and stock.

A three-day fire sale was immediately held at Victoria Hall, when virtually all goods, knitted and woven, and all the stock of wool, were sold at reduced prices.

Then, a long time friend of Nonia, Dr. Harry Roberts, generously offered space in the Centre Building, Church Hill, and for four months, the staff nobly operated from there.

By July, all traces of the fire had been removed and in their well-restored, improved and re-stocked building, the staff was once again able to carry on their fine tradition of service and satisfaction to customers.

NONIA'S HEADQUARTERS – 286 Water Street

Then – 1958 Now – 1990

Nonia Industrial Managers

From its beginning, Nonia has been blessed in having managers who have been both capable and dedicated. Their names, like those of the nurses, deserve to be recorded.

1925-26	Miss Pressley-Smith
1926-27	Miss Leathes
1927-29	Mrs. M. S. Moy
1929-32	Mrs. Lillian Woods
1932-40	Mrs. M. F. Beckett
1940-41	Miss Beatrice Hookey (acting)
1941-73	Miss Beatrice Hookey (became Mrs. Wilfred Moores in 1952)
1973-82	Miss Florence Chafe
1982-89	Mrs. Pamela Dawe
1989-	Mrs. Marilyn Woolridge

The first four named were professionally trained workers from Great Britain.

In 1930 the posts of Industrial Manager and Business Manager were combined.

During her eight year term, Mrs. Beckett insisted upon a very high standard of workmanship for the Outport Centres and of efficient operation at the St. John's Depot.

When Miss Beatrice Hookey was appointed as successor to Mrs. Beckett, she had already worked with Nonia for ten years. As manager she continued to work until her retirement in 1973; her whole working life, forty three years, was devoted to Nonia.

Mrs. Beatrice (Hookey) Moores
(1940 – 1973)

Miss Florence Chafe
(1973 – 1982

Mrs. Pamela Dawe
(1982 – 1989)

Mrs. Marilyn Woolridge
(1989 –)

NONIA MANAGERS
1940 – 1990

Nonia Women's Exchange (1926-1929)

Late in 1926 it was felt by Lady Allardyce that many women in St. John's would like to earn "pin" money to supplement their slender means while others would be willing and able to pay for the things they produced.

The Nonia members and staff predicted that there would be a ready market for such items as pickles and jams, bread, cakes, cookies and salad dressing as well as some articles of plain sewing such as aprons and maids' uniforms.

The price of each article was fixed by the maker and an additional 10% added to cover the cost of running expenses and leave a small profit. Each member was given a number, so that the identity of the seller remained unknown to the purchaser; an annual fee of one dollar was charged.

The operation started slowly but, in the first months, a profit of about $20 per month was made and felt to be worthwhile. The 1927-28 Annual Report showed that the Women's Exchange commissions for the year amounted to $151.77, a worthwhile sum at that time.

In the following year, the commission amounted to only $33.00 and this was the last year in which the scheme operated.

The facilities at the Depot could not cope with breads, cookies and jams which, without proper storage, deteriorated quickly over

Nonia Exchange.

The Women's Exchange dispenses ginger nuts, jam, cream pies, salad dressing, original toys and needle work, etc., etc. The Shrove Tuesday dance sub-committee is alive to its responsibilities and those who mean to play bridge and auction forty fives will please not forget to advise Mrs. Herbert Outerbridge of their intention. She does want them to have a good time, and the kindly Manager of the Newfoundland Hotel will know for how many he must prepare supper if Nonia can tell him how many mean to help her by coming to dance or play cards.

The Evening Telegram

the weekends, so the whole Exchange scheme came to a halt in 1929.

Standards of Excellence (The Impact of Marguerite Beckett)

For nine years, 1931-1940, the Nonia depot manager, Mrs. M. Beckett from England, provided fair but sympathetic criticism of every article submitted for sale; this helped greatly in building up the high standard of workmanship attained by the Nonia knitters and weavers. Mrs Beckett visited every Centre and scores of homes.

From those constructive criticisms, the women of many outports learned that only the best work can receive the best pay. The quality of the knitted and woven goods grew steadily and soon the name Nonia was synonymous with quality in St. John's, Corner Brook, Grand Falls, London and at the Mainland outlets.

Nonia and Knitting

Reference has already been made to Lady Allardyce's firm belief that Nonia could, to a large extent, become self-supporting through the efforts of the outport women, most of whom were skilled in "ordinary" knitting such as socks, mitts, and sweaters; it was only a few years since thousands had knitted for the "boys overseas" in World War I.

Sample garments from the Shetland and Fayre Islands were brought to Fortune Bay by Lady Allardyce while on a visit to the South Coast with her husband. At that time, Fortune Bay was one of the most distressed areas in Newfoundland.

The patterns from the Scottish isles were quickly mastered by the resourceful women of the Nursing

Centres to which they were sent. Soon very marketable articles were being received from Pool's Cove, Hant's Harbour, Rose Blanche and other properly organized centres.

The earliest knitted goods were brought, in a small suitcase, to Government House by Rev. H.J.A. MacDermott. The first sale, a sweater, was made to Lady Outerbridge, wife of Sir Joseph. For the next three years most Nonia knitting was brought to Government House and sold to Nonia members and their friends.

Mr. MacDermott recorded that "when I gave the payment to the first knitter, she looked at the amount—ten dollars—with eyes that sparkled and then filled with tears."

"Every copper a woman earned went into the home; and thus the homes were brighter and children better fed and clothed. The making of patterns and introduction of colours carrIed the women away from a gray and drab life into the brightness of beauty and colour."

From the beginning there was a tendency for certain Centres to specialize in their knitting. For example, the women of Winterton produced intricate pattern pullovers; Salvage, gossamer baby shawls; Islington and Lower Island Cove, beautiful socks; Heart's Content, children's and ladies cardigans.

Today this trend towards specialization still continues as can be seen from the following recently compiled list:

Hare Bay – Ladies' and Gents' Caribou pullovers
Jamestown – Children's Caribou pullovers
Lower Island Cove – Ladies' and Gents' Norwegian pullovers
New Perlican – Children's Fairisle pullovers
Salvage – Ladies' 2 ply cardigan & baby shawl
Robinsons – Norwegian sweaters
Normans Cove – Norwegian sweaters
Thornlea – Norwegian sweaters
Old Perlican – Cable and diamond sweaters
Custards Head – Fancy cable, fine knit wear
Winterbrook – Baby wear
Cavendish – Caps and mitts
Miles Cove – Adult wear
Dover – Accessory knits
Jackson's Arm – Gents' cable trim cardigans
Musgravetown – Children's duffle coats cross over baby sweaters

Knitting (The Life Blood of Nonia)

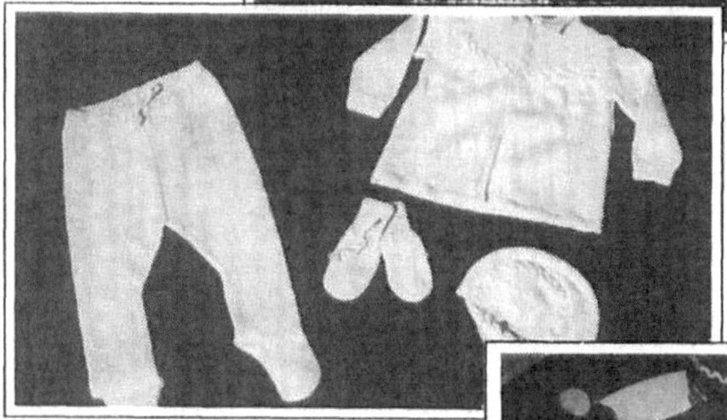

"The stitch of quality that never drops"
(Mrs. W. Moores, 1968)

Special Orders for Knitted Goods

The quality of Nonia knitting was such that, inevitably, special orders were placed. It may be of interest to include a sampling of these; the complete list would be too long.

1957 Newfoundland Pee Wee Hockey team sweaters for a Mainland tournamant.

1961 Caribou design sweaters for Hon. J.W. Pickerskill and family.

Nonia Supporter

This picture was used by Hon. J. W. Pickerskill for his 1960 Christmas card

1963 30 Ladies Sweaters for Standard Manufacturing Company

1970 Convention orders - sweaters for the Fisheries Council of Canada and Master Brewers Association.

1975 15 Sweaters for the Howie Meeker Hockey School

1975 44 Seal design cardigans for the Newfoundland Refinery Company.

1988 200 pairs of ladies' mitts for Squibbs of Montreal

Sweaters for Champions. 1990

For the World Figure Skating Championships held in Halifax, March 5-11, 1990, Aran Fisherman Knit pullovers were supplied by Nonia to the fourteen members of the Canadian Team.
They were made by Nonia knitters from Lethbridge, Dover and Norris Arm South. These ladies must have been very proud to have them worn by such outstanding skaters.

The fact that Mrs. Barbara Ryan, seen at the centre of the group, was not only President of the Canadian Figure Skating Association but also a Board Member of Nonia doubtless had something to do with this substantial order.

1990 Fifteen sets (sweaters, caps, mitts, scarves) for a promotion by Purity Factories.

MacDermott of Fortune Bay
"His parish was the whole field of human need."
Dr. H.M. Mosdell, May, 1938.

Mrs. Hugh MacDermott
For nearly thirty years helped her husband in all his good works, including Nonia.

Nonia and Weaving

Very early in the history of O.N.C. Lady Allardyce was able to add weaving to the already popular knitting program. Sir Wilfred Grenfell, a staunch supporter of O.N.C. and Nonia, offered to send one of his well-trained weavers to initiate a weaving project in a selected community.

Fortune Bay was in dire straits at that time, so Miss Minnie Pike of Red Bay, Labrador, was sent on October 11, 1922 to Pool's Cove. A loom was sent from St. Anthony, and for two months Miss Pike travelled from cove to cove teaching both men and women how to weave. Pool's Cove was an excellent choice, because the Congregationalist clergyman of the area, Rev. H.J.A. MacDermott, and his wife took such an interest in the project; their interest and supervision continued unabated until 1934 when Rev. MacDermott retired after 30 years service in Newfoundland. Mr. MacDermott recorded later that weaving not only provided ready money but led to an increase in sheep raising and the making of looms for home use.

Steady progress was made and the earnings of the weavers in the first two years amounted to more than $4000, a large sum at that time.

Further instructional help was given in 1923 by Mrs. Stansfield, an English volunteer skilled in the art of spinning, dyeing, and weaving; Mrs. Stansfield very generously returned again to give further instruction in the summer of 1924 and 1925.

The Loom Room

By 1925, there were seventeen looms (all made by the men) in use at Pool's Cove, and interest was being shown by some of the other communities such as Garnish, Anderson's Cove and St. Joseph's.

The first weaving classes in Pool's Cove were held in the vestry of the church since no other space was available.

However, when the telegraph office at Long Harbour Tickle (seventeen miles away!) was closed, Rev. MacDermott got permission to dismantle it and the men of Pool's Cove quickly rebuilt it, with changes, to accommodate weaving classes. The Prime Minister, Hon. W. S. Monroe, sent a donation towards the cost of rebuilding, and Nonia funds to the extent of $465.52 were also contributed. It soon became known as the "Loom Room" and was a gathering place for people of all ages.

The first floor of the building consisted of a workroom for weaving and instruction. In this, Mrs.

Stansfield, on her third visit, gave valuable instruction in spinning and dyeing as well as weaving.

Soon a second story was added as a bedroom for women from other communities who wished to take lessons but could not afford to pay for board and lodging.

The Loom Room became really well equipped in 1926 when it received the generous gift of several new looms from the Department of Public Works.

From early Fall until late Spring the Loom Room became the regular meeting place on Wednesday evenings. The women would bring their own work, then a book would be read to them and, finally, the inevitable cup of tea was served

In his report to the Annual Meeting of Nonia in 1927, Rev. H.J.A. MacDermott reported that, in Pool's Cove, 19 looms were in use but only four or five were producing articles for the depot in St. John's. He added, "I am convinced that, in the work done for the people themselves, lies the real value and benefit of the weaving industry."

In an earlier letter to the Secretary of Nonia, Mr. MacDermott had reported that "the underclothing worn by some of the men and boys of Pool's Cove had been woven by the women of the place. The children are wearing the sweaters and jumpers of the patterns and designs of the Association. The women themselves are reaping the benefit of their increased incomes and are very grateful for the opportunity of the work."

In the winter of 1926, Miss K. Williams also gave instruction in weaving at Anderson's Cove; the following summer she taught the women at Garnish.

Miss Daly from St. Joseph's proved to be a very quick learner at Pool's Cove and returned home with

HAND WOVEN IN NEWFOUNDLAND
NONIA
REG'D

Many weaving centres, but Pool's Cove became "Weaving Capital of Newfoundland".

full weaving equipment to pass along her skills to others.

In 1929, the Industrial Manager of Nonia, M.S. Moy, reported that Pool's Cove weaving was continuing to improve steadily and that large quantities of lovely mercerized cotton table runners, beautifully woven and finished, were being received. Pool's Cove was indeed becoming the "Weaving Capital of Newfoundland," thanks to the encouragement and supervision given by the MacDermotts.

From Fortune Bay to Trinity Bay
Miss Beatrice Hookey gives instruction at Clarenville

As can be seen from the accompanying picture, weaving gradually spread to other interested communities, and excellent scarves, placemats, etc., soon started to arrive at the Nonia Depot in St. John's.

In 1965, when Nonia agreed to receive and sell all the work done by the many weavers of the Jubilee

Guilds, extra shelf space and display space had to be provided. In recent years, as craft centres were opened all over the Province, fewer woven goods have been received by Nonia. At present there are seven Nonia weavers, six on Random Island, one in Point Leamington.

Home Hooked Mats

The first home hooked mats came to the St. John's depot from Rencontre East where Rev. MacDermott found that the women were skilled and interested. He was so fascinated by the work of two ladies, Mrs. Matthews and Mrs. Hillier, who were working on a large rug at Bay du Nord that he decided to work out mathematically the number of pull-throughs. The total was 80,000!

The traditional Newfoundland design mats proved most popular; new and original designs were distributed as early as 1928-29 and very attractive mats resulted.

In 1930, the Nonia depot sold more hooked mats than ever before. Many of these came from a beautifully hooked shipment from Stone's Cove, F.B., their first attempt.

By 1933, Mrs. M.F. Beckett, always a perfectionist, was able to report that "With reference to the hooking of mats, this, at many Centres, has reached a stage of perfection. The work is so wonderfully fine and even that, on many occasions, it has been difficult to convince customers that the hooking has been done by hand."

But for the trade depression of those years the market for hooked mats could have been greatly increased. In 1937, Mrs. Beckett reported that "it has not been possible to carry out the mat hooking industry owing to the inability to afford the large outlay necessary to make the undertaking worthwhile."

During the next half century rug hooking has been somewhat spasmodic but the Nonia shop has always had some hooked rugs on display and for sale.

In recent years, the traditional folk art mat hookers of Placentia Bay have become organized under the name Placentia Bay West Mat Hookers.

Nonia continues to stock home hooked rugs with the Newfoundland motif being the popular sellers.

Some of the popular designs used by the Placentia West Mat Makers.

Nonia as an outlet for Grenfell Products

In 1922 Sir Wilfred Grenfell generously assisted Nonia by sending a trained worker to Pool's Cove for two months to instruct the women of the area in the art of weaving.

It was natural, therefore, that Nonia should reciprocate later by acting as a sales outlet for International Grenfell Association products, especially the classic Grenfell cloth and duffle coats many of which feature genuine fox fur trim and hand embroidery.

In addition, Grenfell cloth mitts, tea cozies, tote bags and Grenfell cards find a ready market at the Nonia store.

Other Newfoundland Handicrafts

In addition to the Grenfell products #286 Water Street gradually began to serve as an outlet for many craft workers from all parts of the Province.

In 1973, it was reported that "Customers are now discovering that our stock of other Newfoundland crafts is the best obtainable—pottery from Grand Rapids, wood carvings from Cormack, Labradorite jewellery, fur toys and Raggedy Ann dolls."

Six years later, Miss Chafe reported that "To the end of August, we bought and sold $4000 of Labradorite jewellery, $1000 of T-shirts, $700 of codfish earrings, and Grenfell items, mostly jackets and ski shirts, to the value of $28,000; also dolls, puppets and Newfoundland tartan dolls."

Many of these items were sold to Canadian and American visitors from tour buses that usually included #286 Water Street as a "must" for one of its stops while touring St. John's.

Traditional Newfoundland souvenirs are especially popular—models of fisherman's dories, small articles made from Newfoundland tartan cloth and, recently, prints of the Newfoundland floral emblem, the pitcher plant. Crochet work is also in demand.

As in the knitting and weaving, the emphasis is on quality control when Nonia accepts handcrafted articles for sale.

Well known artist, Carl Stevenson, painted a picture of the Newfoundland Provincial Flower, the Pitcher Plant for the exclusive use of Nonia. He is seen presenting a framed copy to Mrs. Karen Hickman.

The Men of Nonia

Primarily a women's organization, Nonia has nevertheless, had the solid and valuable backing of scores of men of both cities and outports.

In St. John's

From the beginning, the Governor and the Heads of all the Churches were the Patrons and Rev. Canon G. H. Bolt, a charter Board member, served in an advisory capacity on the Executive from 1920 till his death in 1947; he rarely missed a meeting.

The first Nonia Advisory Committee, appointed in 1927, was all male and consisted of Hon. S. Milley, Hon. H. MacPherson, Mr. J. S. Ayre and Mr. T. V. Hartnett.

Among the men who served Nonia in subsequent years in many ways, including those of Hon. Secretary and Hon. Treasurer, were: George R. Cake, W. F. Hutchinson, W. Angus Reid, V. S. Bennett, R. J. Kayser, Fred Ayre, Derek Bowring, F. P. Barnes, Hon. Fabian O'Dea, Ian Reid, Peter Outerbridge, S. E. Goodwin, Dr. Harry Roberts, Dr. Cluny Macpherson, Hon. W. W. Halfyard, Dr. T. Mitchell, Dr. Charles Howlett and Hon. Campbell Macpherson.

Mr. Joe Day of Bowring Brothers Ltd. staff handled all the tedious Customs work of Nonia for many years, a very valuable contribution.

Mr. R. Quick, Manager of the Newfoundland Hotel in the early days, made valuable display areas available and assisted in arranging fund raising events such as Children's Parties and Dances.

Today, through the cooperation of Manager Bruce Turner, a display case of Nonia products is seen by hundreds of guests and visitors at Hotel Newfoundland.

Rev. J. G. Joyce, in 1927, offered to make available on radio station VOWR, a monthly Nonia hour when news of interest could be broadcast to those workers who were able to listen in.

In Corner Brook

In Corner Brook also Nonia was greatly assisted by Mr. E. A. Charlton, International Pulp and Paper Company, Mr. J. C. Fitzgerald (Business Manager), A. Bergeron, Albert Martin, H. O. House, J. A. Basha, J. Coleman, G. Rowe, Ford Neal and many others.

Mr. Wharton, Manager of Glynmill Inn, was also most helpful to the Corner Brook branch by providing a suitable area in the lobby for the display cases filled with Nonia goods.

In the Outports

In the outports many men assisted greatly in the early years in transporting nurses by boat and dog team, in fair weather and foul.

At Pool's Cove some of the men turned up with their wives for instruction in weaving. As they gained proficiency, many of the women wanted their own loom for home use. The machine-made looms used for instruction in the Loom Room were easily copied by the "handy" men of Pool's Cove, as most of them had built their own houses and boats.

Extended reference has already been made to the tremendous contribution made by Rev. H. J. A. MacDermott in organizing and overseeing the weavers of Fortune Bay, especially Pool's Cove. In personal service over a long period, his contribution to Nonia's work was undoubtedly the most outstanding.

In London England

London friends included Captain Victor Gordon, High Commissioner for Newfoundland, Mr. George Emerson, Sir Edgar Bowring, Mr. George Hawes and Col. W. F. Rendell.

Nonia's Auditors

In its earliest years Nonia's accounts were audited, on a voluntary basis, by the well-known firm, Read, Son, Watson and Leith. Later, when Nonia's "books" became quite time consuming, many reports prepared by the generous firm show "Audit Fee at Cost."

Since Mr. Robert Leith's death the annual audit has been done by the following firms:

Clarkson-Gordon Inc.	1972-1975
Warr & Saunders	1976-1985
Bishop & Hogan	1986-1988
Walter P. Miller & Co	1989-

Representatives of all these firms have been most courteous and helpful to the Nonia presidents and managers.

Sir William's Contribution (The "Governor's Chair")

From the time of his arrival, Sir William Allardyce was a staunch friend and supporter of Nonia. In 1926, during a visit to Scotland, Sir William procured a sample sturdy cotter's chair which he felt could be made by the Nonia workers; it would be a source of employment during the winter months.

The chair, which soon became known as "the Governor's chair," was first sent to Bay du Nord and then to Garnish where the men were keen to try their hand.

From the start, there was a ready market and soon the demand was greater than the supply.

Production gradually ceased when all orders had been filled but, while it lasted, many men of Bay du Nord and Garnish considerably augmented their earnings from an uncertain fishery.

In addition, the men also found a ready market for small furniture and wooden toys.

Wholesale Marketing and Sales Outlets

During its seventy year history, Nonia has been able to establish dozens of outlets in Newfoundland and six other provinces. Some of those have been of short duration but most continued to order knitted and woven goods for many years.

Other Provinces

Mary Mundell, Toronto
The Croft, Bracebridge, Ont.
The Teazer, Mahone Bay, N.S.
Thymewood, P.E.I.
W.J. Wilson, Victoria, B.C.
Carl B. Warder, Thornhill, Ont.
Bowrings, Dorval Airport
Angel's Wear and Things, Toronto
The Captain's Loft, St. Andrew's, N.B.
Bowrings, Kitchener, Ont.
The Chatelaine, Laurentian Hotel, Montreal
Maurice Pollock Ltd. Que.
Ada MacKenzie, Toronto
The Palliser, Truro, N.S.
Manor Richelieu Hotel, Que.
The Children's Corner, Westmount, Que.
Children's Colony, Q.E. Hotel, Montreal
Eaton's, Toronto
Little People, Toronto
Just Jane, Toronto

Holt Renfrew & Co., Toronto
Simpsons, Toronto
Young House of Fashion, Oakville, Ont.
Dill's General Store, Waterloo Park, Alta.

Local

Royal Stores, Corner Brook
Glynmill Inn, Corner Brook
Staff House, Grand Falls
Thistledown Shop, Corner Brook
Hudson's Bay Company, Stephenville
Mr. & Mrs. Temple Baird, Grand Falls
Goodyear & House, Corner Brook
Mount Peyton Hotel, Grand Falls

Today Nonia has only two wholesale outlets; Trés Cher and Outport Knits. Both are located in Toronto.

Many of the knitters of Fortune Bay have formed a well organized group known as Pool's Cove Crafts, and accept orders directly for handknitted goods in 100% wool.

Nonia's Mainland Travelling agent

During most of the fifties and for all of the sixties, Miss Kathleen Keegan of St. John's served Nonia as a travelling saleswoman.

While most of her sales were in Ontario, she covered a wide territory and was responsible for thousands of dollars worth of orders for woven and knitted goods. The 1958 Annual Report for example, records that "our mainland travelling agent returned from a successful business trip in which she obtained orders for about $9500 of Nonia products.

Miss Keegan was an outstanding goodwill ambassador for Nonia and it was with great regret that ill health forced her to resign in 1970.

Effects of Confederation

Confederation with Canada in April 1949, caused serious problems for Nonia and it took many months to adjust to them.

For a quarter of a century, there had been no duty on wool from Great Britain; for the same period Nonia wool had been sent to the various Centres free of postage and the finished goods were returned to the Depot also postage free; letters and telegrams were also sent without charge.

Suddenly then, in 1949, Nonia found that it had no concessions as regards postage, and duty had to be paid on all English, American and Belgian wool; as well, there was a Federal Sales Tax.

The increased cost had to be borne by the consumer. However, the extra money that came into circulation as a result of Children's Allowances, Old Age Pensions etc. more than offset the price increases. Before long, in fact, by the end of 1949, sales had picked up and exceeded those of the previous year.

Fiftieth Anniversary Recognized

Anniversary Pins

To mark the fiftieth anniversary (1920-1970) a special pin was designed and several hundred produced.

Three hundred and seventy workers received one of these special pins.

It is very interesting to note that one of the recipients wrote to Nonia headquarters to say that she was the first baby delivered in Daniel's Harbour after the arrival of Nurse Myra (Grimsley) Bennett in April,

1921. Some years later, Nurse Myra taught this "first baby" to knit and she soon became a regular knitter for Nonia.

Government Recognition

The Smallwood Government also recognized and marked the Fiftieth Anniversary in two ways.

A suitably worded plaque was presented by Hon. J.R. Smallwood who had also commissioned Mr. James R. Thoms to compile a short "History of Nonia"; a copy of this excellent booklet was sent to all recipients of the anniversary pin.

Premier Joseph R. Smallwood presents a special plaque to Mrs. Phyllis Winter, to mark Nonia's Fiftieth Anniversary.

PRESENTED TO NONIA
BY THE
GOVERNMENT OF NEWFOUNDLAND IN
RECOGNITION OF ITS 50TH. YEAR IN
THE FIELDS OF NURSING & HANDICRAFTS
1920–1970

Recognition for Service, 1978

At an Executive meeting of Nonia on May 10, 1978, it was suggested that many knitters and weavers deserved recognition for their long and faithful service to the Association. It was unanimously agreed that, for 25 years of service, a suitably worded plaque be awarded; for 50 years of service (and, by that date, several had qualified) a suitably engraved watch would be given.

Up to May 1989, eight watches and 77 plaques have been awarded.

From comments made by the ladies at the time of the presentations and from letters received later it is obvious that these awards are very much cherished by the recipients.

Mrs Clara Maidment

At least two sweaters every month, of the Fair Isle or Caribou design.

Plaques – 25 years

Florence Ash
Nellie Brown
Emily Burgess
Lucy Burrage
Hazel Butt
Elizabeth Biship
Grace Barbour
Annie Balsom
May Ann Balsom
Margaret Bursey
Helena Bauld
Fannie Cramm
Emma Cramm
Mary Ann Curtis
Maber Curtis
Effie Combdon
Minnie Critch
Ivy Collier
Jessie Chaffey
Betty Curtis
Violet Curtis
Effie Dicks
Susie Jane Ennis
Emma Elliott
Theresa Ford
Lillian Green
Esmeralda Greening
Gladys Hodder
Marjorie Horwood
Sadie Howell
Beulah Hutchings
Marie Hayward
Janet Hustins
Leah Hampton
Cavell Hancock
Adelaide Hancock
Minnie Hunter
Ethel Higdon
Mabel Horlick
Hazel Ingram
Emily Jerrett
Josie Johnston
Grace Lane
Ellen Legge
Annie Lane
Annie Morris
Alice Morris
Mildred Moss
Verna Mercer
Mabel Mercer
Marion Mercer
Weaver Mansfield
Emily Maidment
Gwendolyn Matthews
Minnie Moss
Mildred Newhook
Verda Pike
Hannah Parsons
Vera Penney
Emma Penney
Sally Peach
Muriel Reid
Marion Rowe
Phoebe Russell
Nellie Russell
Kate Russell
Mae Rowe
Belle Stirling
Maisie Skiffington
Iris Skiffington
Bessie Thorne
Phoebe Thorne
Margaret Trowbridge
Rachel Vokey
Nina Weir
Annie Wells
Effie Wicks

Watches – 50 years

Laura Ash
Lucy Burrage
Minnie Critch
Minnie Hunter
Annie Lane
Weaver Mansfield
Marion Rowe
Mae Rowe

Silver Picture Frame – 60 Years

Marion Rowe – 1920–1987

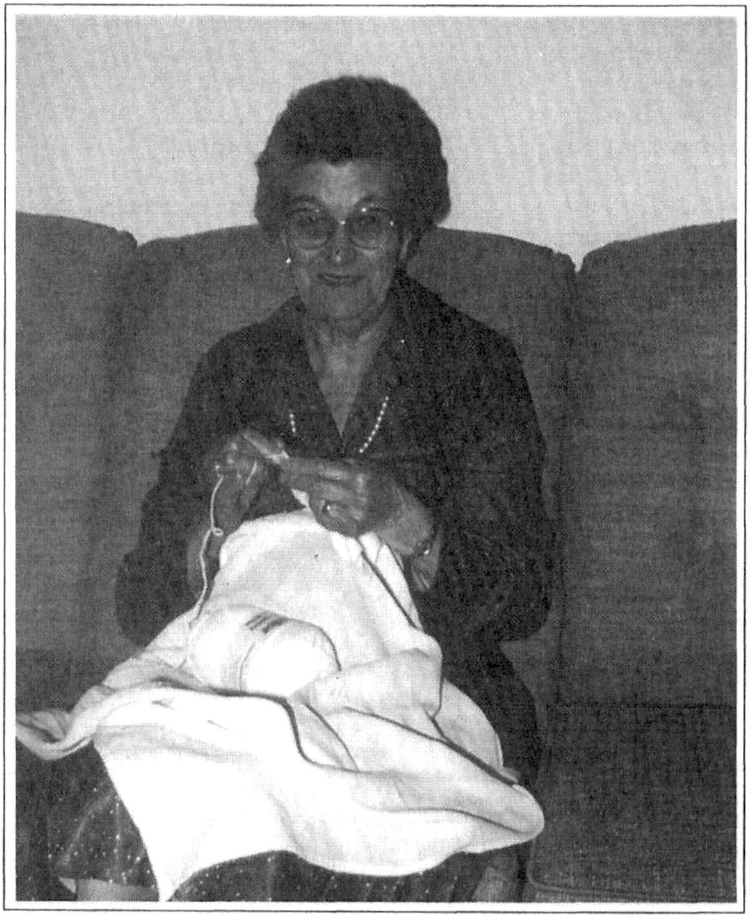

In 1987 Mrs. Marion Rowe of Whiteway was presented with a silver picture frame to mark her 60th year of Nonia knitting; she died in 1989.

1989

50 Years of Knitting

Mrs. Lucy Burrage of New Perlican receives a gold watch.

l–r: Valda Tiller, (Pres); Phyllis Winter, (Past Pres); Mrs. Lucy Burrage; Mrs. Pamela Dawe, (Manager).

Publicity

From the beginning of the outport nursing movement in 1920 there has been solid support from the news media, both the daily press and radio.

Many issues of *The Evening Telegram* and *Daily News* in St. John's carried articles and editorials concerning the nursing and industrial aspects of Nonia. *The Western Star* and *Humber Herald* were also Nonia boosters especially of the Corner Brook District Association.

In the Fall of 1927, just after the opening of Radio Station 8WMC (later VOWR), Rev. J.G. Joyce—whose brain-child VOWR was—offered the use of its facilities to Nonia; soon a monthly one-hour program was being

Original 100 Watt Transmitter on bench. Seated nearby is Rev. Dr.Joyce, with first 500 Watt Transmitter standing on floor.

broadcast, affording an opportunity for Board and staff members to spread Nonia news or send messages to those nurses or workers who were within range.

In those early days of broadcasting few outport homes could afford radios; those that had them, however, generously shared them with friends and neighbors and there were many crowded kitchens when the Nonia hour was being received.

It is interesting to note that, in 1928, when Wesley Church Station obtained remote control equipment, Nonia was honored by making the first broadcast from Government House with Lady Allardyce, Rev. Canon G.H. Bolt and Mr. T.V. Hartnett as speakers on the program.

Starting in 1927, the Saturday edition of *The Evening Telegram* carried a column, under the heading of "Nonia Notes." A scrap book at the Nonia depot contains dozens of these early weekly columns carrying news of interest to nurses, workers and volunteers.

There are also numerous articles by well known columnists such as Jim Thoms, Paul Sparkes, and Sylvia Wigh.

Nonia Notes

NONIA NURSES SLEIGH JOURNEY.

Nurse Dougall's travelling diary as far as Hampden makes interesting reading. She left St. John's on Tuesday February 1st and reached Macgregor's at 8 a.m., where she was met by Elijah Gale and his eighteen dogs. The sleighs were packed and after tea at Gale's father's house they walked as far as Gandy Lake where they got into the sleighs and found it "delightful going across the smooth ice. The dogs found it easier too and never lagged though they required a great deal of encouragement when we were running in snow or up and down banks. It was a lovely day. I had to get out and run every now and then as my feet would get so cold." Sandy Lake was reached at 1 p.m., and at 1.30 another little mail hut where we lunched. Off again at 3 p.m., to reach Stratton's lumber camp at 5 p.m., there twenty-five men live and 'Skipper' Stratton gave up his little room to Nurse, the cook made tea, all were very kind, and Nurse was very comfortable and enjoyed her experience of sleeping in a lumber camp.

On Thursday at 8 p.m. they set out again and this time a hot water bottle dispelled the misery of icy toes. "The road was more difficult for the dogs, continually up and down banks." They passed a number of camps, had cocoa and scones at one, and reached Hampden by noon to be most kindly received by Dr. and Mrs. Creelman, and Nurse Gilliss who is in charge of the little hospital attached to the Doctor's house. Mrs. Creelman was a student at the Halifax School of Art whence come some of Nonia's original designs. She is keenly interested in the people round her new home and with the Doctor has organized an evening school for lads of 14 to 20 years of age 'some of whom do not even know their letters'.

Winter Problems.

Nurse expected to leave on Saturday for Westport but the mailman was ill and she only arrived at her destination on Monday the 14th where she awaited her chance to proceed to Seal Cove. Travelling at this time of the year in Newfoundland gives problems to solve.

From Nonia Notes – *Evening Telegram*, March 19, 1927

Several well-known Canadian daily papers and journals have also published very favorable reviews of Nonia's accomplishments.

Trade Fairs

Participation in local trade fairs not only sold goods 'on the spot' but also spread the word about the quality of Nonia goods, so that many orders resulted.

There was also participation in craft exhibitions in both Canada and England.

For example, the International Grenfell Association invited Nonia to use a section of their stall at the

Empire Exhibition at Glasgow in 1938. In the same year, Mrs. Norbriay, of Sussex Square in London, held an exhibition and sale of Nonia goods at her home; she was a friend of Lady Walwyn.

In 1944 Nonia was asked by the State of New York Branch of the I.O.D.E. to send a selection of goods to a convention being held in New York; the goods were much admired and found a ready sale.

In 1949, Nonia exhibited goods at the Canadian National Exhibition in Toronto and at the Canadian National Station in Montreal to mark Newfoundland's entry into Confederation.

In more recent years, displays are held at the request of convention planners and Nonia garments are worn in some local fashion shows.

Outstanding Service Today

One of Nonia's most faithful friends today is Mrs. Regina McCarthy of McCarthy's Party Tours and Convention Services.

She has directed hundreds of tourists to number 286 Water Street, and substantial sales—especially of knitted goods—have resulted.

Chapter Five

Nonia and the Jubilee Guilds

As early as March, 1961, Lady Outerbridge, Nonia's President, expressed the opinion that "the time has come for Nonia and the Jubilee Guilds to amalgamate; each has a lot to contribute and, together, they could form a strong organization which could benefit the whole island." She reported that she already had conferred with Mrs. Frances Clarke, the President of Jubilee Guilds.

Six months later, on October 24, executive members of both organizations met to discuss this proposed amalgamation.

At that time, Nonia had 423 knitters and 10 weavers; Jubilee Guilds had 230 knitters and 157 weavers.

The two groups did not operate in the same centres. There was a basic philosophical difference in their aims. The main purpose of Nonia was to offer the women of the outports an opportunity to make extra money through their handicrafts; the Jubilee Guilds (1935) were primarily designed to provide a wider outlook through skills and education.

On June 23, 1962, a plan for the amalgamation of the two groups was discussed and it was decided that, since the Jubilee Guilds came under the Department of

Education from which it received considerable financial support, Dr. Alain Frecker, should be informed of the negotiations.

As a result, on April 23, 1962, a meeting of the joint committee had present representatives of both the Department of Education and Economic Development (Messrs. Arthur Johnson, P. J. Hanley, Frank Templeton and Ian MacAllister).

In subsequent months, numerous meetings were held and detailed reports and recommendations were produced. It was not, however, until February 1965, that Nonia, as per agreement with the Department of Economic Development of the Provincial Government, agreed to take over the commercial side of the Jubilee Guilds.

Three members of the Jubilee Guilds Committee, Mrs. Maurice Taylor, Mrs. E. B. Pearce and Mrs. John O'Dea, joined Nonia's Board and were most helpful.

Nonia also took over the many knitters and weavers trained by the Guilds and agreed to market their goods and pay them as they did their own members.

The result of the extra influx of knitted articles and woven goods made it necessary for Nonia to spend several thousand dollars to provide extra storage space on the third floor and to enlarge the display space in the shop area.

So, after three decades of outstanding service to Newfoundland, especially in the teaching of weaving, the Jubilee Guilds were forced to restructure.

Miss Anna Templeton, B.HSc., after thirty years of service as Organizing Secretary (four years) and Supervisor (26 years) was appointed as Director of Craft Training in the newly established Division of the provincial Vocational Education Department in 1965.

Her book on weaving is still regarded as "a veritable bible of the weaving art."

For the next couple of years the Jubilee Guilds retained its name but there was an ever increasing involvement with the program of the well established Women's Institute of Newfoundland and Labrador.

In 1967, Mrs. Frances Clarke became the National President of the Federated Women's Institute of Canada, the first and only Newfoundlander to hold this position. She had also served the Jubilee Guilds for over twenty years, in 1957 as its President.

It was not surprising, therefore, that, at the Provincial Convention of the Jubilee Guilds in August, 1968, a motion was made "that the name of the Jubilee Guilds of Newfoundland and Labrador would be henceforth known as the Newfoundland and Labrador Women's Institutes." After a lively discussion this motion was passed. The name, Jubilee Guilds, will, however, always be associated with a very important chapter in our history. The story of Jubilee Guilds has been well recorded in a 1989 book, *Threads of Gold,* by Agnes M. Richard. (Published by *Creative Publishers.*)

Chapter Six

This 'n' That

What Nonia Has Meant to Me

A SEPARATE VOLUME would be needed to record all the interesting extracts from letters of individuals and reports from Centres. Here are just a few examples, both early and quite recent.

1925 "This work came to be when my heart was sore but my interest deepened as I continued to knit the beautiful wools. Most of the children have their Sunday dresses knitted, done with the wool of their own sheep from the patterns they have learned. I feel I want to have every little outport to have a share in this beautiful work."

1925 "Thanks very much for the bit of money you paid for it; it was something grand. As you know it helped to buy some medicine for her. If our work is good, please don't forget us."

1925 From Rev. H. J. A. MacDermott, Pool's Cove, F.B. "It may be of interest to you to know that the underclothing worn by some of the men and boys has been woven by the women of Pool's Cove. The children are wearing the jumpers and sweaters of the designs of the Association. The women themselves are reaping the benefit of their increased incomes and are very grateful for the opportunity of the work."

Mr. MacDermott also recorded that "one girl found a way open to her, through Nonia, to training in Berea College, Kentucky, for three years before returning to teach." Another used her earnings to attend the London School of Weaving.

In 1926, Nurse Casement (Fowlow) of Rose Blanche reported that an eleven year old girl, deaf and motherless, asked to be allowed to knit to earn money for the Nonia nurse's salary. Her work was good and she was given a continuous supply of wool.

1927 Nurse Hughes in an address to the Annual Meeting, September 19, 1927.

"I remember when the knitting was first started in Garnish and the first payments were made. I paid a woman ten dollars for knitting a fancy sweater. She had tears in her eyes when I paid her the money and said, 'Nurse, this will buy me a barrel of flour.'"

1927 A young knitter from Pool's Cove wrote to say, "I have bought all my school books from money received from Nonia and hope to earn enough to attend the Normal School in St. John's for Teacher Training."

1931 Mrs. L. R. Woods in her Annual Report, "One girl at Winterton who is a cripple and one of our best knitters employs her whole time knitting for Nonia and keeps herself and her family on the proceeds."

1976 From Mrs. Butt, Secretary at Winterbrook "Nonia knitting is still a god-send to a lot of people around the outports especially to women living alone. They like to have something to do and look forward to their parcel of wool every month."

Mrs. John Hiscock of Winterton (at age 80!)
"I would die if I did not have a sweater of the Caribou design to knit for Nonia."

1989 From Mrs. Lucy Burrage, New Perlican
"When I started knitting for Nonia at Whiteway in 1939 it was my only source of income ... when I moved to New Perlican I continued knitting to bring in an extra income for my family of three daughters and one son ... in 1962, I took over as Secretary for New Perlican ... in later years I have knit approximately four or five sweaters a month, one for one of the Queen's sons—a great thrill for me."

When asked how many sweaters she had knitted for Nonia during her more than 50 years of knitting, she replied "I knitted about 3200 garments."

Nonia Visitors Book (1932 – 1951)

What a pity that this record did not start as soon as the first depot was opened in the Reid Newfoundland Building in 1924 and continue until the present. However, the book was in use during the years of Depression, the Commission of Government, World War Two and the early years of Confederation.

On its pages are the names of many well known visitors from Church and State, and those of scores of officers from the army, navy and air force of Great Britain, United States and Canada; these men were very pleased to be able to find, at the NONIA outlet, suitable gifts for wives and girl friends.

There are also several names of well known entertainers and movie stars who visited the U.S.O. Centres in Newfoundland to entertain the troops. For example, Joan Blondell of Los Angeles, California recorded her name on October 12, 1942.

Visitors' names from all Canadian provinces and most of the United States can be seen, and many added complimentary remarks. Perhaps the most welcome and happiest was made by well known Corner Brook businessman Ford Neal, on July 19, 1944. It was brief and to the point, "Now she's paying—finally!"

Generous Donors

During its early years, in fact, until it had reached the mid "teens," Nonia was the recipient of many generous gifts both in cash and in goods.

The following is a partial list of the major donations received during the thirteen years between 1925 and 1938.

1920 - 1927	Overseas Nursing Assn. to each nurse at time of embarkation	£20
1924	Lord Rothemere	$2000
	Reid Nfld. Company	$1000
	Her Majesty the Queen	£10
1927	"Sympathy"	$ 300
	W.I. Bishop, Montreal	$ 300 towards rent
	Lord Rothemere	$1000
	A.E. Harris	$ 200
1928	Sir Joseph & Lady Outerbridge	$ 400
	Lord Rothemere	$2500
	H.J. Crowe	$ 236.70
1929	Colonial Missionary Society	£200 per year for three years
1930	Lord Rothemere	$1000
1931	International Pulp and Paper Co.	$1000

1932	International Pulp and Paper Co.	$1000
1936	U.K. Branch of Nonia	$671.65
1938	Anglo Newfoundland Development Co.	$250
1939-40	Anonymous (towards tonics for needful children)	$200

Gifts in kind included supplies of cod liver oil for the Nursing Stations from W.A. Munn, Job Brothers, A.P. and W.P. Goodridge; boxes of apples from a Nova Scotia orchard, 150 beautifully made garments from Lady Thomson of London as well as much new and used clothing from the London Branch.

By 1940, Nonia seems to have matured to the point where it could balance its books without assistance. However, during the succeeding years, there have been many thoughtful gifts from friends and supporters.

For instance, in 1946, through the St. John's Royal Trust Company a generous donation was received from Miss Emily Harris of England. This resulted from the sale of etchings by her late brother, a well-known artist who retired to live and work in Brigus, C.B. after retiring as manager of the A.N.D. Company of Grand Falls.

In 1959, Mrs. Harold Mitchell, donated a new typewriter and $300 towards Christmas advertising; and, in the 1962-63 year, Lady Outerbridge imported a generous quantity of Irish linens and Madeira work which she donated to be sold at the Nonia store for extra profits.

The Story of the Silver Casket

In April 1928, Lady Allardyce, as founder and Number One Booster of the work of Nonia, was presented by the members with a handsome miniature silver casket, suitably engraved. It was a token of appreciation for all that she had done.

After Lady Allardyce died in England, the casket disappeared, but nearly thirty years later, it was accidentally found in London.

Captain Art Lindhop, an Air Canada pilot had been stationed in St. John's during his career; he was, therefore, familiar with Nonia.

While browsing through an antique shop in London, he spotted the casket and, realizing that Nonia in Newfoundland would be interested, made a deposit on the casket. On his return to Canada, the Captain contacted Mrs. Gerald Winter who thanked him profusely and "spread the word" about the lucky find. As a result, Hon. Campbell Macpherson, the former Lieutenant-Governor,generously purchased the casket and, after having had it refurbished, presented it to the Association.

It is now displayed for all to see at the Association's depot at #286 Water Street.

Mrs. Phyllis Winter, President of Nonia in 1972, receives the silver casket from Hon. Campbell Macpherson who retrieved it, thanks Captain Lindhop, and had it completely refurbished before presenting it to Nonia.

M.V. "NONIA"

Nonia's first President in the late twenties, Lady Elsie Allardyce, dreamed of having a small vessel owned by and named *NONIA*. The boat would carry supplies to many centres and take the finished articles back to St. John's. This dream was never realized. However, many years later, in 1956, the high esteem in which Nonia was held by the people of Newfoundland was such that a new coastal passenger vessel operated by the Government was named "NONIA."

M.V. *NONIA* – 1956
"Good luck to her Captain
Good Luck to her Crew"

At the launching of the vessel in Aberdeen on April 10, 1956, the following telegram was sent by the staff at Nonia in St. John's.

To: Mrs. Philip Gruchy
(wife of the Manager of the Anglo Newfoundland Development Company, Grand Falls.)
c/o Capt. M. A. Dalton
c/o Hall Russell & Co.
Aberdeen, Scotland

Both sides of the water
Today drink this toast
Good fortune to "NONIA"
When sailing our coast
Good luck to the Company
Good luck to you
Good luck to the Captain
Good luck to the Crew.

From
Nonia H.Q.
St. John's

NONIA
and
the Royal Family

1925 A generous donation of £300 from the London Branch of Nonia included £10 from Her Majesty the Queen.

1927 Nonia held a knitting competition for the best knitted baby garment. Her Royal Highness, the Duchess of York, graciously accepted a beautiful little coat and cap knitted by Mrs. Ethel Brown and Mrs. Tessier as a gift for the baby, Queen Elizabeth.

1928 At an exhibition of Nonia goods at the Forum Club in London, Her Royal Highness, Princess Louise, requested that Nonia workers be told that she considered their work "to be beautiful and of a very high standard."

1932 Quite recently Nonia was honoured by a second order from H.R.H. the Duchess of York for lengths of vislaine for herself and H.R.H. Princess Elizabeth.

1937 Queen Elizabeth attended the London Forum Club exhibition of Nonia goods and purchased 27 yards of tweed to be made into coats for the young princesses.

As a result of this visit, Royal permission was given for Nonia to use the words, "As supplied to Her Majesty the Queen."

1937 "I do wish the Newfoundland workers could have seen and heard the Queen. She was so deeply and sincerely interested, so appreciative of the workmanship and eager to help them practically with suggestions and ideas." (Letter to Nonia H.Q. from Lady Allardyce)

1941 H.R.H., the Duke of Kent, at the London Forum display of Nonia goods, bought sweaters for Prince Edward and Princess Alexandra.

1947 A six yard length of hand woven material to H.R.H. Princess Elizabeth on the occasion of her marriage. Her reply, "I can assure you that your choice is one that has given me real pleasure and I ask you to thank all concerned for their kindness, generosity and goodwill."

1948 A generous length of hand woven tweed was sent to H.R.H. Princess Louise.

1970 To mark Nonia's 50th anniversary the Royal Family accepted the gift of sweaters for the Prince of Wales, Princess Anne, Prince Andrew and Prince Edward. (The Royal Family indicated that they would like heavy-knit sailing sweaters and specified the colours.)

1987 Government House presented a Nonia knit Norwegian style sweater to Prince Andrew when he visited.

1988 On June 8th, when Prince Edward unveiled the plaque to open Prince Edward Plaza on George Street in St. John's, he too, was presented with a Nonia sweater.

Notable Quotes (from the early years)

Bishop William White, 1925

"When it is remembered that Nonia stands "for earning power" with its consequent comforts to the homes and persons of hundreds of our people, gratitude for the inspiration which made such things possible takes possession of one's soul."

Lady Elsie Allardyce, First Presidential Report, June, 1925

"Nonia may be likened to a toddling child, eager and wistful, at times full of beauty and promise, other times faulty, stumbling and weary. Its little hands carry healing and promise to many. Shall we help it grow?"

Sir Wilfred Grenfell, April, 1926

"I can guarantee that the work of Nonia is constructive, business-like and a true message of the Gospel of Love without any distinction or reference to race or creed. It is really helping to clothe the naked, feed the hungry, heal the sick and preach the Gospel of Love."

Most Reverend E.P. Roche D.D., Archbishop of St. John's

(From letter to Nonia, 1926.)

"Besides the practical work done the spirit of Nonia is to develop and encourage habits of thrift and industry, and I hope its influence will become more widespread year by year."

Letter from Bartle C. Frère, September 9, 1926

(attended annual meeting of Nonia in St. John's – "Calvert House")

"May the vital energy and posturing care infused by Lady Allardyce and her already many helpers spread from week to week, till the necklace of devoted ladies that encircles the shores of Newfoundland is complete and all minds are freed from financial anxieties about so priceless a boon."

Jim Thoms (in his booklet on Nonia)

"Lady Walwyn dived into the work."

Lady Allardyce, 1928, when leaving Newfoundland

"May Nonia continue to grow in courage, faith and strength and lighten the burdens so that new joy and security may reign in Newfoundland."

Lady Allardyce (in "Nonia Notes" – a weekly column in the "Evening Telegram")

"In a few hours His Excellency and I shall leave the shores of the Island, our Home for five years and four months ... your Narrows were a tiny entrance to a wide world of happiness and service."

The Famous Amulree Commission Report, 1933

"We have nothing but admiration for the untiring energy and devotion with which a small band of voluntary workers have sought by all means in their power, to further the interests of their less fortunate compatriots in the outports. We would hope that the industrial side of the Association will be kept in being."

Nonia Scholarships

In 1982 the Executive of Nonia decided to institute a scholarship program for first year students, male or female, in the fibrecraft courses being offered at the Craft Training School in St. John's.

Since that date seven annual scholarships, valued at $500 each have been awarded as follows:

1982	Miss Roberta Dale
1983	Miss 'Jackie' Crummey
1984	Miss Janice Young
1985	Mrs. Lois Verfaille
1986	Miss Nadine Mills
1987	Miss Cindy Chafe
1988	Miss Lisa Burke
1989	Mrs. Donna Stagg
1990	Miss Wendy Coombs

Better than any other organization, Nonia recognizes the value of handicrafts to the economy of the Province and this annual scholarship is evidence of its support of training in fibrecrafts.

The $500 scholarship is tenable at the Avalon Community College, St. John's or an equivalent institution.

March 23/88 – The *Evening Telegram*

Miss Lisa Burke receives the $500 Nonia scholarship from Her Honor Mrs. Margaret McGrath, the Honourary Patroness of Nonia. On the left is President Valda Tiller and on the right Mrs. Carol Matthews, Second Vice-President

Government House Hospitality
The Birthplace of Nonia

It may not be generally known that the idea of outport nursing, partly supported by cottage industry, was conceived at Government House, that it was born there and that, in its early years from 1920 to 1924, it had its home there.

The first four Presidents, from 1920-1944, were the wives of Governors; from 1960-1966, Lady Dorothy Outerbridge, wife of Lieutenant Governor, Sir Leonard, served as an outstanding President and generous supporter.

In the early years, Government House was the site of scores of committee meetings. Apart from two Annual meetings held at Canon Wood Hall and the Newfoundland Hotel, the remaining sixty eight have been convened at Government House.

The early meetings were presided over by His Excellency, the Governor or his wife. At the most recent meeting His Honour, the Hon. James McGrath, expressed the hope that "This tradition of holding Nonia's Annual Meeting at Government House will continue throughout the Nineties and beyond."

Looking Ahead
Nonia in the Nineties

For the last thirty two years, Nonia has been operating successfully from #286 Water Street, its fifth home since it was founded in 1924.

At the 1990 Annual Meeting, President Valda Tiller reported that "although our financial statement is not as attractive as we would hope, our auditor assures me that the business is quite stable. With so much competition in the craft business, it is difficult to keep sales up; however, our high standards of quality ensure a superior product."

Mrs. Valda Tiller
President (1986–)

The Association has a keen Executive made up of sixteen members headed by Mrs. Valda Tiller, now in her fifth year as President.

NONIA Board of Directors

Annual Meeting, Government House, March 1990

Front Row: L–R Mrs. Lorraine McLoughlan, Mrs. Karen Hickman, Mrs. Valda Tiller, Mrs. Phyllis Winter, Mrs. Paula Collingwood.

Back Row: L–R: Mrs. Carol Matthews, Mrs. Barbara Ryan, Mrs. Sonya Ryan, Mrs. Virginia Bell, Mrs. Loretta Martin, Mrs. Diana Andrews, Mrs. Karen Viscount, Miss Janice Udell, Mrs. Cheryl Westaway, Mrs. Janet Andrews, Mrs. Karen Misik.

The present staff consists of six dedicated members whose average length of service is nine years. The manager, Mrs. Marilyn Woolridge, though comparatively new to Nonia, is highly skilled and making her presence felt.

NONIA Staff, 1990

Back Row: L–R Cathy Marsh, Marilyn Woolridge, Lorraine Field, Florence Gosse.

Front Row (seated) L–R Eileen Williams, Betty Pitcher.

Nonia continues to be a non-profit organization in the sense that its main objective is to pay a fair price to its many craft workers and also a fair salary to the members of its staff at the Water Street depot. When annual returns permit it, a bonus is paid to the knitters and weavers.

Nonia does not receive any government subsidy.

There are at present 25 Industrial Centres in operation, 240 knitters and seven weavers. Top quality goods are arriving steadily, sales are good, and the outlook is a bright one.

Despite the tremendous technological advances of this century, it seems that there will continue to be a steady and universal demand for high quality, home-produced knitted and woven goods, Grenfell jackets and the many other products of Newfoundland and Labrador "cottage" industries.

With annual sales of goods in the past decade approaching closser and closer to the $400,000 mark, everything points to a bright future for Nonia in the nineties and beyond.

Bibliography

Talks by: Mrs. Phyllis Winter
Mrs. C.E.A. Jeffrey

Nonia Annual Reports 1925-1990

"Born to Serve" J. R. Thoms

Evening Telegram Editorial, March 2, 1956
April 10, 1956

Evening Telegram column, March 26, 1955
Mrs. C.E.A. Jeffrey

Atlantic Guardian, June 8, 1957

Atlantic Guardian, January, 1957

Daily News, June 20, 1960

Newfoundland Journal of Commerce, July, 1963

Newfoundland Quarterly, 1935 (Summer)

Newfoundland Who's Who? 1930, 1932

"Nonia", *Spring Echoes* Mary G. Bray

Scrap book of clippings *(Evening Telegram)*
Nonia Notes 19—. 19

Books of Newfoundland (Vol II) J. R. Smallwood

Nonia Visitors' Book (1933-1951)

Newspaper Clippings, November 13, 1926, May 12, 1928

Brief Histories of Nonia: Mrs. Loretta Martin
Mrs. T. Mitchell
Mrs. Phyllis Winter

Report from Rev. H.J.A. MacDermott, 1921 (Oct.)

"Among the Deep Sea Fishes" (I.G.A. Magazine), April 1926

MacDermott of Fortune Bay
(Biography of Rev. H.J.A. MacDermott) 1938

Threads of Gold Agnes M. Richard (Creative Publishers, 1989)

Files of Nonia's Fiftieth Anniversary, 1970

White Caps and Black Bands Joyce Nevitt

"Nonia" by Joseph Rutledge
(International Paper Nonthly, March 1928)
copied from Toronto *Financial Post*